Potato People

44 of the Best Potato Recipes for Potato Lovers

By Kelly Scott

TABLE OF CONTENTS

INTRODUCTION

In the culinary world, there is nothing more versatile than the potato. From the thousands of different kinds of potatoes (and yes, there are thousands of different varieties) to the thousands of different dishes you can make with potatoes, you will never get bored of eating them. Whether mashed, roasted, fried, or baked, this tuber has found its way into every person's heart and every culture.

If you ask me what my favorite food is, my answer is always the potato. Whenever someone asks me what my last meal on earth would be if I had a choice, I always list off at least three different kinds of potatoes. There is not a day that goes by when I don't eat a potato, and if there is, that is the day I am dead. This book is a compilation of my favorite potato recipes, for all those who are potato people too. I hope you enjoy cooking these potato dishes, from tried and true classics to new and fun recipes inspired by potato dishes around the world. Bon appétit!

DIFFERENT KINDS OF POTATOES

There are well over 5,000 different potato varieties in the world. Over 4,500 of those varieties are located in South America alone. Unfortunately, for the rest of us in the world, we don't have as much access. So, in this book, we will be cooking up the varieties that you will most definitely have access to!

DIFFERENCE BETWEEN WHITE AND SWEET POTATOES

White potatoes (such as Russet and Yukon Gold) and sweet potatoes (often orange-fleshed or sometimes purple) belong to different plant families and have distinct nutritional profiles, flavors, and textures. Here are some key differences between white potatoes and sweet potatoes:

White Potatoes:

- Belonging to the Solanaceae family, which also includes tomatoes, peppers, and eggplants.
- White potatoes typically have light tan to brown skin and white to yellowish flesh.
- White potatoes have a neutral to slightly sweet flavor and a starchy texture.
- White potatoes are much higher in starch.
- Rich in complex carbohydrates, particularly starch, they are a good source of vitamin C, potassium, and vitamin B6.
- White potatoes generally have a higher glycemic index compared to sweet potatoes, leading to a quicker spike in blood sugar levels when consumed.
- Commonly used for baking, frying, mashing, and boiling, they are versatile in savory dishes.
- More commonly consumed in North America and Europe.
- Examples include Russet, Yukon Gold, Fingerling, Kennebec, and Red Potatoes.

Sweet Potatoes:

- Belonging to the Convolvulaceae family, which is unrelated to white potatoes.
- Sweet potatoes come in various colors, including orange, purple, and white. The skin can range from beige to orange or purple.
- Sweet potatoes have a naturally sweet flavor, especially when cooked, and a softer, creamier texture.
- Sweet potatoes are much higher in moisture content.
- High in beta-carotene (which gives them their orange color), a precursor to vitamin A, they are also a good source of fiber, vitamin C, manganese, and potassium.
- Sweet potatoes tend to have a lower glycemic index, resulting in a slower and more sustained release of glucose.
- Suited for roasting, baking, mashing, and in both sweet and savory preparations, they are often used in casseroles, pies, and as a side dish.
- Popular in many parts of the world, especially in Asia, Africa, and the Americas.
- Examples include Japanese Sweet Potato, Yams, White Sweet Potato, Okinawan, Hannah, and Garnet.

Notes on Sweet Potatoes vs. Yams

I want to clarify the difference between sweet potatoes and yams since it can be confusing. In the U.S., we refer to the orange potatoes as sweet potatoes, which is technically incorrect. Sweet potatoes and yams are both in the sweet potato family because they are both sweet. However, yams are the orange potatoes we think of when we think of sweet potatoes. Sweet potatoes are actually white. In my recipes, I will call them by their technical names, so don't be thrown off by that. However, some titles, such as "Sweet Potato Fries," might seem confusing because they call for yams. I did this because when you think of sweet potato fries, you think of the bright orange fries. But these are yams, so they will state that in the ingredient list.

In summary, just know that we get technical in the ingredient list, not in the title!

Notes on Salting

You will notice in all of my recipes that, for the most part, I do not specify the amount of salt you should use; it will usually say "salt to taste." This is because when it comes to seasoning, there are many different factors determining how much salt is the right amount for you. First and foremost, I do not know how much salt YOU like. Each person's taste buds are very different and sensitive when it comes to salt. For example, I absolutely love salt and will add it to everything, including my water! My mom, however, prefers things less salty, so whenever I cook for her, I have to tone it down a lot. Knowing your own preferences when it comes to salt is important.

The second factor is that the amount of your other ingredients may vary slightly. The potatoes you choose might be larger or smaller than the ones I use in the recipes. Now, this is totally okay because in my recipes, I teach you to go by texture, flavor, and consistency, rather than blindly following a recipe. So you will be able to adjust accordingly, but this is why seasoning on your own based on flavors is an important skill to develop. If the sweet potato you chose was smaller than the ones I used, and I tell you to use 2 tsp of salt, it could be horribly over salted! We want to avoid this at all costs.

Instead, I recommend you follow the steps when I say to salt and season in these recipes. You will notice you want to salt in layers and throughout the cooking process. Salting throughout the recipe allows salt to cook with the food and enhance flavors. Salting just at the beginning or just at the end of some recipes will result in unevenly seasoned dishes. Don't be afraid to constantly taste what you are making; your taste buds are what are going to tell you if you need to add salt throughout. You should never be tasting and thinking "wow, that was salty," but instead look for the ingredients to be enhanced and brightened by salt.

This is a skill that, once you practice and develop it, will be important and useful in everything you cook. So don't be afraid to salt!

Notes on Oil

You will notice that many of my recipes will not give the exact amount of oil. This is because there are many variables when it comes to oil use, whether you are oiling potatoes in a bowl or adding oil to your sauté pan.

When you are coating potatoes in a bowl, you should go based on what you see. What I mean is, are the potatoes evenly coated? Do some look dry? Then add oil. Do they look like they are drowning in oil? Then drain some out. We have to learn to trust our senses. If I were to give you an exact amount of oil for a recipe, and your potato just happens to be smaller than the ones I use, then your potatoes will be drowning in oil because it would take more for me to coat my potatoes since they are bigger. For this reason, we trust our senses and what we see.

The same goes for when we are adding oil to a pan. I usually won't give an exact amount because I do not know the size of the pan you are working with. If I worked with an 11-inch sauté pan and you are working with an 8-inch sauté pan, you are going to need a lot less oil than I will. Go by the instructions such as "evenly coat the bottom of the pan," or "add enough oil so it is 5 inches high in the pan."

Much like knowing how much salt to use, this is a skill you develop. Practice makes perfect!

White Potatoes

Burnished Potatoes

I know it is crazy to start my potato book with a British potato dish when I am constantly saying the French have the best potatoes... yet here we are! Burnished potatoes are the best roast potatoes you will ever have: crispy, fluffy, and infused with garlic and rosemary.

INGREDIENTS

- 4 russet potatoes, peeled and cut into large 2-inch chunks
- Salt and pepper
- ½ cup olive oil
- 5 cloves of garlic, crushed
- 3 sprigs of rosemary

DIRECTIONS

1. Preheat the oven to 425°F.
2. In a pot of salted water, boil the potatoes for 8-10 minutes, until you can just barely pierce them with a fork. Drain and let them sit for 10 minutes until dried.
3. Place the oil in the pan you are going to use for the potatoes. Add the garlic and rosemary, and heat in the oven for 5 minutes. Remove the pan from the oven and coat the potatoes in this oil, along with salt and pepper.
4. Add the potatoes to the pan, making sure they are spread out, and roast for 20 minutes. After 20 minutes, flip them over and roast for another 20 minutes or until crispy. Remove and enjoy!

Pommes Purre

Pommes purée is just a fancier way to say mashed potatoes. And if you are making mashed potatoes not from an instant bag, then congratulations—you are fancy af. If you are looking for the smoothest, silkiest, buttery mashed potatoes, then these are for you.

INGREDIENTS

- 2 lbs gold potatoes, peeled and cubed into 1-inch cubes
- Salt, to taste
- 1 cup heavy cream or coconut cream if you are dairy free
- 3 sprigs thyme
- 1 sprig rosemary
- 3 garlic cloves, smashed
- 1 stick of butter, cubed and at room temperature or cool
- White pepper to taste

DIRECTIONS

1. Heat the oven to 400°F.
2. Bring a pot of water to a boil and add enough salt to make it taste like the sea. Add your potatoes and boil until they are very soft and fork-tender, about 15-25 minutes. Once soft, strain through a strainer.
3. Add the potatoes to a parchment-lined sheet tray and bake in the oven for 10 minutes. This will dry out the remaining water.
4. While the potatoes are in the oven, steep the cream. Add the cream to a pot with the rosemary, thyme, and garlic and bring to a low simmer. Steep for 5-10 minutes to infuse the flavor, then strain out the herbs and garlic.
5. Press the hot potatoes through a fine mesh strainer or ricer into a bowl. This may take a while, but it is worth the super fine texture.
6. Add half of the hot cream to the strained potatoes, and half of the cubed butter. Mix with a spatula until smooth. Add more cream and the remaining butter as needed. Taste and add salt and white pepper to taste. Serve immediately.

Smashed Potatoes

If you like super crispy, cheesy potatoes, then these are for you. A smashed potato is kind of just what it sounds like: a small potato boiled, smashed, and roasted until crispy. The uneven edges make for crispy cracklings that you won't be able to stop eating.

INGREDIENTS

Potatoes:
- 2 lb small gold or red potatoes
- Salt and pepper, to taste
- ½ cup olive oil
- 1.5 cups Parmesan cheese, finely grated
- 1 tsp Italian seasoning
- ½ lemon, juiced

Garlic Aioli:
- 2 egg yolks
- 4 garlic cloves, grated
- ½ tsp salt
- ½ lemon, juiced
- 1 cup avocado oil

DIRECTIONS

1. Preheat the oven to 400°F.
2. Bring a pot of water to a boil and season heavily with salt. Add the potatoes and boil for 10-20 minutes, until they are fork-tender. Strain and allow them to air dry for 5-10 minutes.
3. On a cutting board or flat surface, smash the potatoes using a bench scraper or flat object. Place them on a parchment-lined sheet tray with an inch of space between each potato.
4. In a bowl, mix together the olive oil, Parmesan cheese, Italian seasoning, juice of ½ lemon, and salt to taste. Brush this mixture onto each potato, on both sides.
5. Transfer the tray to the oven and bake for 20 minutes. Remove from the oven and flip each potato over. Bake for another 10-20 minutes until they are golden brown and crispy.
6. While the potatoes are in the oven, make the aioli. Add the yolks, salt, garlic, and lemon juice to a container that you can use with an immersion blender. Mix before adding the oil.
7. With the immersion blender running, slowly add the oil, a drizzle at a time, to emulsify it with the yolks. Continue blending and adding oil until the aioli is very thick.
8. Serve the potatoes with the aioli and enjoy!

Potato Pave

Potato Pave

Potato Pave is the fanciest recipe in this book, and also one of the best. Potato pave is a French dish that consists of thinly sliced potatoes layered in a baking dish with butter and cream, then baked until tender and golden. It is finished by frying until crispy and delicious. This dish takes two days to prepare, so definitely plan ahead for this one.

INGREDIENTS

- 1 cup heavy cream or coconut cream
- Salt and pepper, to taste
- 3 garlic cloves, crushed
- 4 sprigs thyme
- 2 sprigs rosemary
- 3 russet potatoes
- 5 Tbsp butter, diced into small cubes
- Avocado oil for frying

DIRECTIONS

1. Preheat the oven to 350°F.
2. In a pot, combine the cream, salt, pepper, thyme, and rosemary. Bring to a very low simmer and steep for 15-20 minutes to infuse flavor, ensuring it doesn't bubble over. Turn off the heat and set aside.
3. Peel the potatoes and thinly slice using a mandolin. The slices should be thin enough to easily bend. Trim them to fit into a 10x5 inch sheet tray lined with parchment paper.
4. Start layering the potatoes in the tray: place a layer of potatoes, brush with the infused cream, sprinkle with cubes of butter, salt, and pepper. Repeat until all potatoes are used. This task requires patience but is worth it!
5. Fold the parchment paper over the potatoes and cover with foil. Bake in the oven for 1 hour and 50 minutes.
6. Remove from the oven, uncover, and let cool for 30 minutes. Line with foil again, place a weight on top to press down, and refrigerate for 24 hours.
7. Remove from the fridge, carefully transfer to a cutting board, and cut into desired shapes (rectangles, squares, or triangles).
8. In a nonstick pan or cast iron skillet over medium heat, add enough avocado oil to create a thin layer. When the oil is hot, add the potatoes, cut side down, and fry until golden brown on each side, approximately 3-5 minutes per side.
9. Remove from the pan, let cool for 5 minutes, and serve. Enjoy!

Lyonnaise Potato

Lyonnaise potatoes are often overlooked, but they might be in my top five favorite potato recipes in the book. They are a classic French dish featuring thinly sliced potatoes cooked with onions until both are golden and tender. The onions are caramelized to perfection, which truly elevates this dish to a 10/10.

INGREDIENTS

- 1 lb small gold potatoes, thinly sliced
- 1 onion, julienned
- 4 Tbsp clarified butter
- Salt and pepper, to taste
- 2 Tbsp fresh thyme leaves

DIRECTIONS

1. Bring a pot of water to a boil. Add a generous amount of salt, so it is salty but not as salty as the ocean. Boil the potatoes for 3-5 minutes, or until slightly tender. Drain and set aside.
2. While the potatoes are boiling, heat 1 Tbsp of clarified butter in a large stainless steel pan over medium heat. Add the onions and caramelize them, stirring occasionally with a wooden spoon. This will take 20-30 minutes. Deglaze with water as needed if dark brown spots form on the pan. Turn the heat to low midway through cooking. Add salt towards the end once the onions are caramelized. Turn off the heat and remove the onions.
3. In a cast iron or nonstick pan over medium heat, add 3 Tbsp of clarified butter. Once warm, add the potatoes and stir occasionally, allowing them to get golden brown on each side, which takes roughly 10-15 minutes. Once golden, add the caramelized onions, thyme, and pepper. Taste for salt and season accordingly.
4. Serve and enjoy!

Pommes Anna

Pommes Anna is a classic French dish featuring dozens of layers of thinly sliced potatoes, butter, and herbs baked under weight to create a crispy potato dish. This labor of love is totally worth it, as it turns out gorgeous at the end!

INGREDIENTS

- 4 lbs russet potatoes
- ¼ -½ cup clarified butter, melted
- Salt and pepper, to taste
- 5 garlic cloves, grated
- 2 tsp Italian seasoning
- Maldon salt for garnish

DIRECTIONS

1. Preheat the oven to 425°F.
2. Peel the potatoes and thinly slice them on a mandolin; you want them as thin as possible. Place the slices in a bowl and coat them evenly with melted butter or oil, salt, pepper, grated garlic, and Italian seasoning.
3. Arrange the potatoes in a 10 inch nonstick pan or cast iron skillet, brushing some butter or oil on the pan first. I like to arrange them in circles starting from the middle. Layer the potatoes one at a time, continuing until you run out of potatoes.
4. Top the potatoes with parchment paper, then place a heavy oven-safe object like a pot on top. This weight helps press down the potatoes, creating a crispy crust and ensuring even cooking.
5. Bake in the oven for 25 minutes. Remove from the oven, take off the weight and parchment paper, and return to the oven for another 15 minutes to brown the top.
6. Remove from the oven and carefully flip the dish onto a plate. Let it sit for 10 minutes to cool slightly. Slice and serve! I like to sprinkle some flaky salt or herbs on top as well.

French Fries

There is nothing worse than a soggy French fry. They are far too common for my liking, which is why I love to make them at home. By boiling them first and then doing a double fry, you will have the crispiest fries ever!

INGREDIENTS

- 2 large russet potatoes, washed and cut into fry shapes
- 2 Tbsp cornstarch
- 4-6 cups avocado oil, for frying
- Salt, to taste

DIRECTIONS

1. Bring a pot of water up to a boil and season heavily with salt. Add the potatoes and boil for 3 minutes. This removes excess starch and will allow potatoes to get crispy. You don't want to cook them too much, just until they are partially cooked but mostly still raw. Remove from the water and dry with paper towels.
2. Add the potatoes to a bowl and coat with cornstarch.
3. Add the oil to a fryer or pot. Bring up to 335°F. Once it is up to heat, work in batches to not overcrowd the fryer and add the potatoes a handful at a time. Fry for three minutes and then remove. Do this with the remaining fries.
4. Once all the potatoes are blanched (step 3), raise the temperature of the oil to 375°F. Add the potatoes once hot, working in batches to not overcrowd the pan. Fry for 3-5 minutes or until golden brown and crispy. Remove the fries from the hot oil and immediately transfer to a bowl. Season with salt and toss. Repeat this with the remaining potatoes.
5. Serve and enjoy!

Garlic Parmesan Fries

There are many French fry recipes in this book, but I dare say these garlic parmesan fries are the best. They are as good as, if not better than, most restaurant fries!

INGREDIENTS

- 2 batches of French fries
- 2 Tbsp butter
- 10 cloves garlic, minced
- ½ cup Parmesan, freshly grated
- 2 Tbsp parsley, minced

DIRECTIONS

1. Follow the instructions for the French fries and make them.
2. For the garlic butter, add the butter to a small pan over medium heat and melt it. Once it starts bubbling, add the garlic and turn off the heat. This will cook the garlic. Stir in the Parmesan and parsley, then set aside.
3. Once the French fries are cooked and in a bowl, add the garlic herb butter and toss until evenly coated. Serve and enjoy.

Animal Style French Fries

In-N-Out wishes they could make Animal Fries as good as these! No, seriously, these are 100x better than theirs. With caramelized onions, secret sauce, cheese, and the crispiest fries, these are a crowd-pleaser.

INGREDIENTS

For the Fries:
- 1 batch of French fries
- 4 American cheese slices

For the Onions:
- 2 Tbsp butter
- 1 onion, diced
- Salt and pepper, to taste

For the Sauce:
- ¾ cup mayo
- ¼ cup ketchup
- 3 tsp yellow mustard
- 2 Tbsp relish or chopped pickles
- Salt and pepper, to taste

DIRECTIONS

1. Follow the instructions for the fries and make them.
2. Cook the onions. In a stainless steel pan over medium heat, add the butter. Once melted, add the onions and caramelize them. Stir frequently until the onions are golden and caramelized. Deglaze with water as needed if spots on the pan get dark brown. Towards the middle of cooking, turn the heat to low. Add salt towards the end once the onions are caramelized. Caramelizing the onions will take 15-30 minutes. Remove from the heat once they are golden and set aside.
3. For the sauce, whisk together all of the ingredients. Taste and adjust the seasoning accordingly.
4. Add the fries to a baking sheet and top with the cheese. Place under the broiler in the oven for 3 minutes, until the cheese melts. Remove from the oven.
5. Plate the fries. First, add the fries, then top with the onions and the sauce. Serve and enjoy.

Poutine

Poutine might be the ugliest potato dish in the world, but it's the most popular Canadian dish for a reason! I can rarely find it gluten-free when eating out, so I've been making it for myself for years. Since most of y'all don't live in Canada and have access to it, it's time to try making it at home.

INGREDIENTS

- 1 portions of French fries

Gravy Ingredients:

- ¼ cup butter
- ½ onion, minced
- 1 carrot, minced
- 1 celery rib, minced
- Salt and pepper, to taste
- ¼ cup all-purpose flour or gluten-free flour
- 2.5 cups beef broth
- 1 Tbsp tamari or soy sauce
- 2 sprigs thyme

Toppings:

- 1 cup cheese curds

DIRECTIONS

1. Prep the fries and set aside, but don't fry the fries until step 6.
2. Prepare the gravy. In a pot over medium heat, melt the butter. Once the butter is foaming, add the onion, celery, and carrot. Sauté until translucent, about 5-8 minutes, salting as you go.
3. Once the vegetables are cooked, sprinkle in the flour and coat the vegetables. Cook for another 2-3 minutes.
4. Slowly stir in the beef broth, whisking in a little at a time to avoid lumps. Add the soy sauce and thyme, then season with salt and pepper. Bring to a simmer and cook for 20 minutes to thicken and develop flavor.
5. Strain the gravy through a fine mesh strainer and set it aside.
6. While the gravy is cooking, fry the fries.
7. Assemble the poutine. Place the fries on a plate, smother with gravy, and top with cheese curds. Serve and enjoy!

Shoestring Fries

And the crispiest potato in this book goes to these Pommes Pailles—also known as Shoestring Fries! They are also the easiest fry recipe since you don't have to double fry them. They are thin enough to get crispy in one go!

INGREDIENTS

- 2 russet potatoes
- 4-6 cups Avocado oil for frying
- Salt, to taste

DIRECTIONS

1. Peel the potatoes and, using a mandolin set to ⅛-inch strips, slice them into shoestring pieces. Place the slices in a bowl of ice water and soak for 30 minutes to remove excess starch. Strain and dry on paper towels once ready.
2. Add oil to a fryer or pot and heat to 375°F. Once the oil reaches the proper temperature, work in batches to avoid overcrowding the fryer, adding the potatoes a handful at a time. Fry for 3-5 minutes, then remove.
3. Transfer the fries from the oil to a bowl and immediately season with salt. Repeat with the remaining fries and serve immediately.

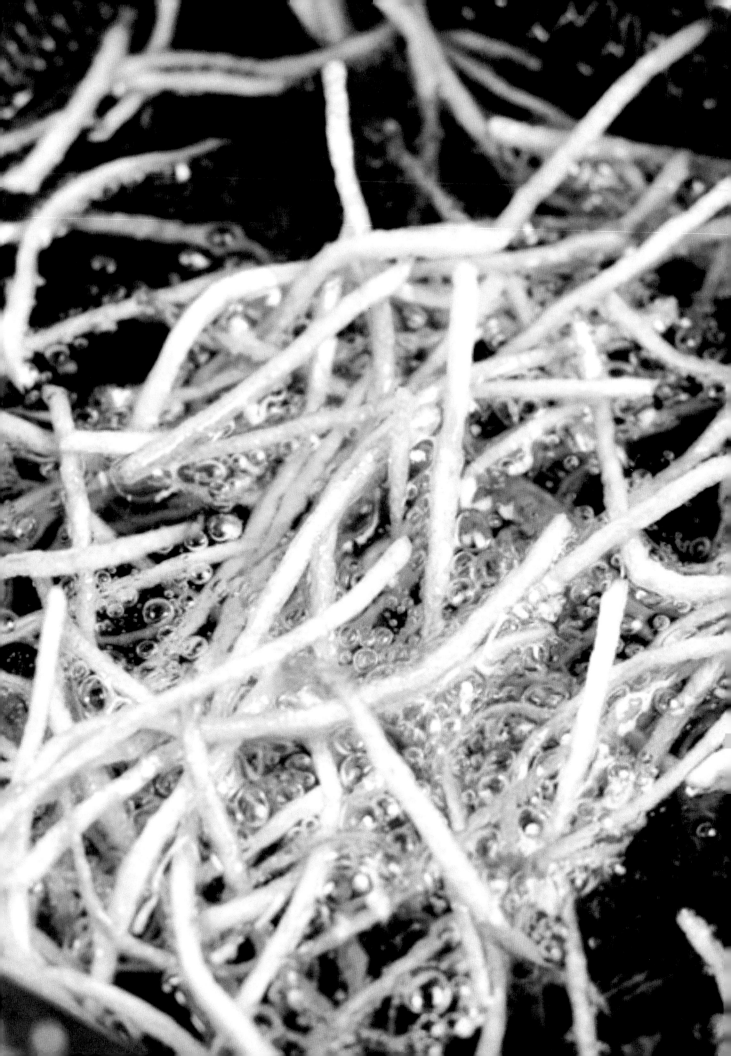

Potato Croquettes

If you are a fan of fried food and mashed potatoes, meet your new favorite dish. Croquettes are mashed potatoes that are breaded and then fried. Although they are a labor of love and take some time, they are definitely worth it. Even make the mashed potatoes a day before to save some time!

INGREDIENTS

- 2 cups pommes purée, cooled
- 2 tsp chives, minced
- ½ cup Parmesan cheese, grated
- Salt and pepper, to taste
- 1 cup gluten-free 1-to-1 flour or all-purpose flour
- 1 large egg
- 1 cup gluten-free panko breadcrumbs or regular breadcrumbs
- 4-6 cups Avocado oil, for frying

DIRECTIONS

1. In a bowl, mix the mashed potatoes with the chives, Parmesan cheese, and salt and pepper to taste.
2. Prepare the breading station: In one bowl, add the flour and season with salt and pepper. In another bowl, add an egg and whisk with one tablespoon of water until smooth. In the third bowl, add the panko breadcrumbs.
3. Roll the potato mixture into 1-2 inch balls and place them on a parchment-lined sheet tray.
4. Dip each potato ball into the egg wash and coat it all over. Roll it in the flour so it is evenly coated, then dip it again into the egg wash. Finish by rolling it in the breadcrumbs, and place it back onto the parchment-lined sheet tray. We first dip it into the flour because the panko will adhere better to the balls, so don't skip this step in the breading process.
5. Add the oil to a fryer or pot and heat it to 375°F. Once it reaches the proper temperature, work in batches to avoid overcrowding the fryer and add the potato balls 2-3 at a time. Fry for 3-5 minutes, or until they are golden brown. Remove them and place them onto a roasting rack over a sheet tray so they don't get soggy. Repeat with the remaining potato balls.
6. Cool for 5 minutes and serve!

Duchess Potatoes

Duchess potatoes are perfect for when you're feeling extra fancy! They are a classic French dish made by mixing mashed potatoes with eggs, piping them into elegant designs, and baking them until golden brown and pillowy soft!

INGREDIENTS

- 1 lb russet potatoes
- Salt and pepper, to taste
- 2 oz butter, room temp
- 2 egg yolks, beaten
- 1 egg, beaten for egg wash

DIRECTIONS

1. Preheat the oven to 400°F.
2. Peel and cut the potatoes into large pieces, then boil in salted water until fork-tender. Drain and dry them on a sheet pan and place in the oven for 10-15 minutes to remove excess water.
3. Using a potato ricer, rice the potatoes. If you don't have a ricer, use a masher. Season with salt and pepper, add the butter and egg yolks, and stir until smooth. Add more butter if needed to achieve the desired mash texture.
4. Transfer the mixture to a piping bag and pipe it into your desired shapes onto a sheet pan lined with parchment paper. Brush lightly with the egg wash. Bake for 12-15 minutes, or until the tops are golden brown and crispy. The baking time may vary based on your oven, so adjust as needed.
5. Remove from the oven and serve immediately.

Latkes

I know I've said this before, but this might be my favorite recipe in the whole book. Latkes are a deliciously crispy Jewish potato pancake. The combination of potatoes, onions, eggs, and flour results in a simple yet delicious dish that you won't be able to stop eating.

INGREDIENTS

- 2 large russet potatoes
- 1 onion
- 2 large eggs
- 2 tsp salt
- 1 tsp pepper
- 1 tsp baking powder
- ½ cup gluten-free 1-to-1 flour or all-purpose flour
- Avocado oil, for frying
- Maldon salt for garnish

DIRECTIONS

1. Using a grater with large holes, grate the potatoes and onion. Working in batches, transfer the mixture to a towel or dish rag and squeeze out as much liquid as possible. Add the drained potatoes and onions to a large mixing bowl.
2. In the same bowl, add the eggs, flour, salt, pepper, and baking powder. Stir until thoroughly combined.
3. In a cast iron skillet or Dutch oven over medium heat, add a half inch of avocado oil. Once the oil is hot, use a tablespoon to drop potato balls into the oil, working in batches and leaving a few inches of space between them. Use a metal spatula to flatten the balls. Cook until the edges are golden brown, then flip and cook until the second side is golden brown as well, which usually takes around 4-5 minutes per side. Remove the cooked balls and place them onto a paper towel-lined sheet tray or cooling rack to drain the excess oil. Top with Maldon salt immediately. Repeat with the remaining batter.
4. Serve and enjoy!

Boulangere Potatoes

Boulangère potatoes are a French potato dish that's essentially a casserole made with potatoes, onions, and stock. I like to bake it and then slice it like a pie to serve. Enjoy this elegant casserole!

INGREDIENTS

- 2 Tbsp olive oil
- 1 onion, julienned
- Salt and pepper, to taste
- 3 garlic cloves, minced
- 2 Tbsp cold butter, plus 4 tbsp cold butter
- 5 gold potatoes, peeled and thinly sliced on a mandolin
- 3 sprigs sage, minced
- 1.25 cups chicken stock, heated
- ½ cup Parmesan, grated

DIRECTIONS

1. Preheat the oven to 350°F.
2. In a large stainless steel pan, add olive oil and heat over medium heat. Once warmed, add the onions and sauté until cooked through, stirring every few minutes and seasoning with salt as you go. This takes around 10 minutes. Add the garlic and sauté for another 2 minutes. Turn off the heat.
3. Butter a 9-inch baking dish and begin the layering process. Layer the potatoes so they overlap each other, then add onions, minced sage, salt, and pepper. Repeat with 3-4 layers until you have used up all the ingredients or filled the dish.
4. Pour the hot stock over the potatoes so it almost submerges them, but the top layer should remain exposed. Top with herbs, additional salt and pepper, and 3 tbsp of butter. Cover with foil and bake for 30 minutes.
5. After 30 minutes, remove the foil and bake for an additional 30 minutes.
6. Remove from the oven and top with Parmesan cheese. Return to the oven and bake for 10 more minutes.
7. Let cool for 10 minutes before serving.

Fondant Potatoes

No, these are not scallops, even though they look just like them. These are fondant potatoes, a fancy French potato dish often seen in fine dining. Seared and then braised in a flavorful liquid, this dish is perfect if you want to impress a date or guests!

INGREDIENTS

- 4 russet potatoes, peeled and cut into 1-inch rounds
- 10 garlic cloves, smashed
- Salt and pepper, to taste
- Avocado oil
- 4 Tbsp butter
- 2 sprigs rosemary
- 4 sprigs thyme
- ½ cup chicken stock

DIRECTIONS

1. Preheat the oven to 400°F.
2. Peel the potatoes, trim the ends, and cut them in half crosswise to yield 8 flat potato rounds. Use a ring mold to cut into rounds. Place the rounds in a large bowl and cover with cold water. Soak for 20 minutes.
3. Arrange the oven rack in the middle of the oven.
4. Drain the potatoes, rinse them with cold water, and pat them dry with paper towels. Season with salt and pepper.
5. Heat oil in a pan over medium-high heat. Add the potatoes, cut side down, and brown for 7 minutes. Flip the potatoes and decrease the heat and add garlic, butter, thyme, and rosemary. Cook until the butter is foaming and starts to brown, about 2-3 minutes.
6. Add chicken stock until the potatoes are half submerged. Bring to a simmer and season with salt. Taste to ensure the liquid is seasoned correctly and adjust accordingly.
7. Transfer to the oven and bake until the potatoes are fork-tender and lightly browned on all sides, about 15-20 minutes.
8. Garnish with additional thyme and drizzle with the pan juices before serving.

Pommes Aligot

Pommes Aligot is a cheese lovers dream potato dish! It's a creamy, cheesy potato dish known for its smooth, stretchy texture. The name "aligot" comes from the word "ali" which means "to bind," referring to the dish's stretchy consistency.

INGREDIENTS

- 1 lb gold potatoes
- Salt and pepper, to taste
- ¼ cup butter, cold and cubed
- ½ cup heavy cream
- 1 sprig rosemary
- 3 garlic cloves, crushed
- ½ cup Gruyère cheese, grated

DIRECTIONS

1. Bring a pot of water to a boil and salt generously.
2. Peel the potatoes and cut them into 2-inch cubes. Add to the boiling water and cook until the potatoes are tender and cooked through, about 15-20 minutes. Drain the potatoes through a strainer and return them to the pot. Place the pot over medium heat and stir with a spatula for 1-2 minutes to evaporate any excess water.
3. While the potatoes cook, in a separate bowl, heat the heavy cream with the rosemary and garlic cloves until it reaches a low simmer. Steep for 15 minutes to infuse the flavor.
4. Rice the potatoes through a potato ricer until smooth. Return the riced potatoes to the pot and place over low heat. Gradually add the hot cream and cold butter, stirring in a little at a time until a smooth, mashed consistency is achieved.
5. Stir in the cheese gradually, allowing it to incorporate and melt. Stir vigorously until all the cheese is fully incorporated. The aligot should form long, stretchy strands when lifted from the pot.
6. Serve and enjoy!

Scalloped Potatoes

Another win for the French with this recipe! Dauphinoise Potatoes, also known as Scalloped Potatoes, are thinly sliced potatoes cooked in a creamy, cheesy sauce. Perfect for a potluck or holiday!

INGREDIENTS

- 2 lbs russet potatoes
- 4 cups heavy cream
- 3 garlic cloves, smashed
- 3 sprigs thyme
- 2 sprigs rosemary
- ⅛ tsp freshly ground nutmeg
- Salt and pepper, to taste
- 1 Tbsp butter, cut into small pieces
- 1 cup Gruyère cheese, finely grated
- 1 cup Parmesan cheese, finely grated

DIRECTIONS

1. Preheat the oven to 400°F.
2. Peel and thinly slice the potatoes using a mandoline to ⅛-inch thickness.
3. Place the potatoes in a pot and cover with heavy cream. Add the garlic, thyme, rosemary, nutmeg, and salt and pepper to taste. Be sure to taste the cream; it should be well-seasoned, or the final dish may be under seasoned. Bring the pot to a low simmer and cook for 20 minutes, until the potatoes are slightly tender.
4. Butter a 10-inch baking dish or large pie pan with 1 tbsp of cold butter. Using a slotted spoon, transfer half of the potatoes into the baking dish, then sprinkle with half of the cheese. Add the remaining potatoes and pour in just enough of the cream to barely cover them. Top with cheese.
5. Transfer to the oven and bake for 40-50 minutes, until the top is golden brown.
6. Remove from the oven and cool for 10 minutes before slicing and serving.

Thyme Potato Torte

If you're a carb lover like me, then this recipe is for you. It's essentially a pie with multiple layers of creamy, cheesy potatoes in the middle. The flaky homemade crust takes it to the next level and is unlike any pie you've had before.

INGREDIENTS

Pastry Crust Ingredients:

- 3 cups all-purpose flour or gluten-free 1-to-1 flour
- 1 tsp salt
- 1.25 cups cold butter, cubed
- ¼ cup to ½ cup ice-cold water

Filling:

- 3 sprigs fresh thyme
- 1 sprig rosemary
- 3 garlic cloves, crushed
- 1 cup heavy cream
- 3 russet potatoes, peeled and thinly sliced using a mandolin
- Salt and pepper, to taste
- 1 cup grated Gruyère cheese
- 1 egg, whisked

DIRECTIONS

1. Preheat the oven to 375°F.
2. Make the pie dough. In a food processor, combine the flour and salt by pulsing a few times. Add the cold butter and pulse until the butter is in small pieces, about the size of small beans. Turn on the food processor and add 2-4 tbsp of cold water, one tablespoon at a time, until the dough comes together. Stop once the dough has formed.
3. Flour your counter and turn the dough out onto it. Using your hands, shape the dough into a disk, then wrap it in plastic wrap. Refrigerate for 30 minutes before rolling out, or up to two days in advance. If refrigerating for longer than 30 minutes, let it sit at room temperature for 5-10 minutes before rolling out.
4. Flavor the cream for the filling. In a pot, add the thyme, rosemary, garlic, and heavy cream. Bring to a low simmer and steep for 10 minutes to infuse the flavors. Discard the herbs and garlic, then set the cream aside.
5. On parchment paper or a counter dusted with flour, roll out the dough to a thickness suitable for pie. Measure with a pie tin to ensure you have an extra 2 inches beyond the edge of the tin. Cut out two rounds. Fit one round into an 11-inch buttered pie tin, trimming any excess dough. Save the second round for the top. Refrigerate the bottom crust for 30 minutes.

Thyme Potato Torte

6. Layer the potato slices in circles on the bottom of the pie crust. Once the first layer is complete, season with salt, pepper, and a sprinkle of cheese. Continue layering with the remaining potatoes until the pie is filled. Pour the cream over the pie until it reaches just below the top layer. Top with the remaining Gruyère cheese.

7. Cover the pie with the second pie crust. Crimp the edges or press with a fork, and trim any excess dough. Make a few cuts in the top crust to allow steam to escape. Whisk the egg and brush the egg wash over the crust.

8. Bake in the oven for 1 hour. If the edges of the pie crust start to brown too much, cover them with foil. Remove from the oven and let cool for 25 minutes before slicing.

Thyme Potato Torte

6. Layer the potato slices in circles on the bottom of the pie crust. Once the first layer is complete, season with salt, pepper, and a sprinkle of cheese. Continue layering with the remaining potatoes until the pie is filled. Pour the cream over the pie until it reaches just below the top layer. Top with the remaining Gruyère cheese.

7. Cover the pie with the second pie crust. Crimp the edges or press with a fork, and trim any excess dough. Make a few cuts in the top crust to allow steam to escape. Whisk the egg and brush the egg wash over the crust.

8. Bake in the oven for 1 hour. If the edges of the pie crust start to brown too much, cover them with foil. Remove from the oven and let cool for 25 minutes before slicing.

Chateau Potatoes

Chateau potatoes are small potatoes cooked in butter, rosemary, and garlic—the perfect combination! The butter browns and helps form a delicious golden crust on the potatoes.

INGREDIENTS

- 1 lb small gold potatoes
- Salt and pepper, to taste
- ¼ cup butter
- 1 sprig rosemary
- 4 garlic cloves, smashed

DIRECTIONS

1. Peel the potatoes and set them aside.
2. While peeling the potatoes, bring a pot of water to a boil and season generously with salt. Add the peeled potatoes and cook for 12-15 minutes, until they are slightly tender but not fully cooked. Strain the potatoes and pat them dry with a towel.
3. In a cast iron skillet or non-stick pan, melt 3 tbsp of butter over medium heat. When the butter is foamy, add the potatoes and begin to sauté. Season with salt and pepper, and add the rosemary sprig and crushed garlic for flavor. Sauté until a golden brown crust forms, about 10 minutes, and the potatoes are cooked through.
4. Once cooked, transfer the potatoes to a serving platter and pour the butter over them. Serve immediately.

Twice Baked Potatoes

I never understood the hype around twice-baked potatoes until I started adding bacon to them. Now, I can't get enough! Loaded with cheese, bacon, bacon fat, and sour cream, they aren't the lightest potatoes, but they are definitely the richest.

INGREDIENTS

- 4 russet potatoes
- 1 lb bacon, sliced
- ½ cup milk
- ½ cup sour cream
- ½ cup cheddar cheese, shredded
- Salt and pepper, to taste
- Minced chives, for garnish

DIRECTIONS

1. Preheat the oven to 400°F.
2. Wash the potatoes and poke holes in them. Place the potatoes on the middle rack of the oven, and place a sheet tray on the bottom shelf to catch any drips. Bake for one hour, or until fork-tender. Remove from the oven and let cool.
3. While the potatoes are baking, cook the bacon. In a large cast iron skillet or sauté pan, add the bacon slices to a cold pan. Turn the heat to medium and render out the fat. Stir the bacon bits with a wooden spoon and cook until crispy. Turn off the heat and remove the bacon bits, draining them on a paper towel. Save the bacon fat.
4. Slice the potatoes in half and scoop out the flesh into a bowl. Place the potato shells on a parchment-lined sheet tray.
5. In the bowl with the potato flesh, add 3 tbsp of bacon fat and stir until smooth. Add the milk and sour cream, and stir until combined. Stir in the cheese, half of the bacon bits, and season with salt and pepper to taste.
6. Spoon the filling back into the potato shells, mounding it slightly. Transfer to the oven and bake for another 10-15 minutes, or until warmed through.
7. Garnish with the remaining bacon bits and chives before serving.

Hash Browns

There are many ways to shape hash browns, but my favorite is the Waffle House style. For those wondering wtf Waffle House is, it's only the best breakfast spot in the Southeast. And by "best," I mean it's perfect at 2 AM after a night out. Their hash browns come out in one giant circle on a plate, just like the ones here.

INGREDIENTS

- 3 russet potatoes, peeled
- 1 onion, grated
- 2 eggs, whisked
- ¾ cup gluten-free flour, all-purpose flour, or cornstarch
- Salt and pepper, to taste
- ¼ cup clarified butter

DIRECTIONS

1. Grate the peeled potatoes using a box grater or food processor. Soak the grated potatoes in ice-cold water for 30 minutes to remove excess starch.
2. Strain the potatoes and place them in a clean kitchen towel or cheesecloth. Squeeze out as much moisture as possible. This step is crucial for making the hash browns crispy, so try to remove all the water.
3. In a large bowl, combine the grated potatoes, chopped onion, eggs, flour, and salt and pepper. Mix well.
4. Heat the clarified butter in a large skillet over medium-high heat.
5. Once the butter is hot, take a large handful of the potato mixture and press them into a patty. Place the patty in the hot butter, pressing down slightly with a spatula. Cook the hash brown for about 5-8 minutes per side, or until they are golden brown and crispy.
6. Once both sides are golden and crispy, transfer the hash brown to a plate lined with paper towels to absorb any excess oil. Repeat with the remaining potato mixture.
7. Serve and enjoy!

Tartiflette

Tartiflette is possibly the richest potato dish in the world and isn't for the faint of heart. Popular in France, Tartiflette is a potato casserole with layers of potatoes, bacon, caramelized onions, wine, and is topped with a generous amount of cheese.

INGREDIENTS

- 2 ½ lbs gold potatoes
- Salt and pepper, to taste
- ¼ lb thick-cut bacon, diced
- 1 Tbsp olive oil
- 2 onions, julienned
- ½ cup dry white wine
- ½ cup heavy cream
- 3 fresh thyme sprigs, leaves removed
- 1 pound Reblochon-style cheese or brie, sliced into ½-inch slices

DIRECTIONS

1. Preheat the oven to 375°F.
2. Peel the potatoes and slice them into ¼-inch slices. In a pot of boiling water, add salt and the potatoes. Simmer for 4-5 minutes until they are just barely tender but not fully cooked through. Drain the potatoes and set them aside.
3. In a large sauté pan, add the bacon and turn the heat to medium. Render out the bacon fat, and once the bacon is golden, remove it and set aside.
4. In the same pan, over medium heat, add the onions. Sauté until the onions are cooked through, salting as you go. Deglaze with the white wine and bring it to a simmer. Reduce until it is nearly dry, then mix in the heavy cream and thyme. Bring to a simmer for 2 minutes, seasoning with salt and pepper to taste. Turn off the heat.
5. In a 9x9-inch pan, arrange the casserole. First, layer half of the potatoes on the bottom, then half of the bacon, and then half of the cream mixture, spreading the onions evenly. Repeat with the remaining potatoes, bacon, and cream mixture. Top with the wedges of Reblochon cheese.
6. Transfer to the oven and bake for 30-40 minutes, until the cheese is bubbling.
7. Remove from the oven and cool for 10-15 minutes before serving.

Tartiflette

Spanish Tortilla

Although this is technically an omelet, I had to include it in this book since it is one of Spain's best potato dishes. A Spanish tortilla is a simple tapas dish consisting of eggs, potatoes, and onions cooked in olive oil. It is great both as a breakfast, a snack, or a tapas.

INGREDIENTS

- ½ cup olive oil
- ½ lb gold potatoes, peeled and cut into thin slices
- ½ onion, julienned
- 6 eggs
- Salt, to taste

DIRECTIONS

1. In an 8-inch non-stick pan, add the olive oil and heat over medium heat. Add the potatoes and cook, stirring occasionally. After 3 minutes, add the onions and salt. Cook until the potatoes are fork-tender. Strain through a fine-mesh strainer.
2. In a separate bowl, whisk the eggs. Add salt and the potato mixture, and mix with a spatula. Let it sit for 10 minutes to thicken.
3. In the same pan over medium heat, add a few tablespoons of olive oil and pour in the eggs. Cook for about 10 minutes, or until the top barely jiggles. Flip the omelet onto a lid, or plate, and slide it back into the pan. Cook for another 2 minutes.
4. Slide the omelet out of the pan onto a plate and serve.

Patatas Bravas

Patatas Bravas are Spain's gift to the world... well, that and paella. Patatas Bravas are crispy potatoes served with a Spanish paprika-based sauce. They are traditionally served as tapas, though I could easily eat a whole plate of them myself!

INGREDIENTS

- 4 russet potatoes, peeled and cut into 2-inch cubes
- 2 Tbsp cornstarch
- Avocado oil
- Salt, to taste
- ¼ cup olive oil
- 2 tsp Spanish smoked paprika
- 1 tbsp gluten-free flour or all-purpose flour
- 1 cup chicken stock

DIRECTIONS

1. Boil a pot of salted water and add the potatoes. Boil for 3 minutes to remove excess starch that could make them soggy. Drain and dry on paper towels.
2. In a bowl, add the potatoes and coat in cornstarch. This will make them extra crispy.
3. "Blanch" the potatoes: Add avocado oil to your fryer and set the temperature to 325°F, or heat oil in a pot on the stovetop to 325°F. Once heated, work in small batches to avoid overcrowding the pot. Fry the potatoes for 3-5 minutes, just until slightly cooked through. Remove and set aside. Repeat with the remaining potatoes.
4. Between the first and second rounds of frying, prepare the sauce. In a pan over medium heat, add ⅔ cup olive oil, 1 tbsp paprika, and 2 tbsp flour. Whisk for 2-3 minutes. While whisking, gradually add the chicken stock and combine. Bring to a low simmer and continue whisking for another 10-15 minutes to cook out the raw flour flavor and thicken the sauce. Season with salt to taste.
5. Once the first round of blanching is complete, increase the fryer temperature to 375°F. When the oil is heated, fry the potatoes in batches until golden brown, around 3-5 minutes. Remove and immediately place them in a bowl and salt.
6. Top the potatoes with the bravas sauce and serve.

Batata Harra

Batata Harra is a delicious Lebanese potato dish packed with flavor from various spices. If you are looking for a potato dish that packs a punch, this is a must-try.

INGREDIENTS

- 6 gold potatoes, cut into 1-inch cubes
- Salt, to taste
- ⅓ cup olive oil
- 6 garlic cloves, minced
- 1 tsp ground coriander
- 1 tsp ground cumin
- ½ tsp smoked paprika
- ¼ tsp crushed red pepper flakes
- ½ cup cilantro, chopped
- ½ cup dill, chopped
- 1 lemon, juiced

DIRECTIONS

1. Preheat the oven to 425°F.
2. In a pot of salted water, boil the potatoes for 8-10 minutes, until you can just barely pierce them with a fork. Drain and let them sit for 10 minutes until dried.
3. Add the potatoes to a bowl and coat them with a light amount of olive oil and salt. Lay them on a parchment-lined sheet tray and roast in the oven for 30 minutes, until golden brown.
4. In a large sauté pan over medium heat, add the remainder of the olive oil. Once warm, add the garlic, coriander, cumin, and paprika, crushed red pepper flakes and sauté for 2 minutes until fragrant.
5. Stir in the potatoes and coat them with the mixture. Turn off the heat once coated. Stir in the fresh cilantro, dill, and lemon juice. Serve and enjoy!

Gnocchi

Many people would argue that gnocchi is more of a dumpling or pasta dish, but I would argue it is a potato dish at its core! It is my favorite to make because it is quite easy to make gluten-free and still tastes just as good as the gluten version.

INGREDIENTS

- 2 lbs russet potatoes
- 1 cup 00 flour or gluten free 1-to-1 flour
- 1 egg, whisked
- 1 tsp salt

DIRECTIONS

1. Preheat the oven to 375°F.
2. Poke the potatoes with a fork all over. Place them on a sheet tray and bake in the oven for 45 minutes to 1 hour, or until they are soft, fork-tender, and cooked through. Baking instead of boiling dries out the potatoes, allowing for better texture in the gnocchi.
3. Peel the skin off the potatoes and discard it. Push the potatoes through a ricer. If you don't have a ricer, push them through a fine-mesh strainer.
4. Dust your countertop with flour. Place the riced potatoes flat onto the surface and coat with 1 cup of flour. Mix together with your hands. Add the whisked egg and salt, and knead the dough just until a ball forms. Cut into quarters. Add more flour if the dough is too wet.
5. Working with one section at a time, roll the dough out with your hands until it is 1/2-inch thick. Using a bench scraper or knife, cut into small pieces. Set aside and dust with flour so they won't stick together.
6. Cook the gnocchi. Bring a large pot of salted water to a boil. Add the gnocchi, working in batches to not overcrowd the pot. Once the gnocchi floats to the top, remove them with a slotted spoon.
7. Finish in sauce of choice and serve.

Greek Lemon Potatoes

The Greeks know what they are doing when it comes to potatoes. These wedged potatoes are cooked in a delicious sauce of lemon juice, garlic, chicken stock, and herbs to make perfectly fluffy and delicious potatoes.

INGREDIENTS

- 3 large gold potatoes, cut into long wedges
- ⅓ cup olive oil
- ½ cup chicken stock
- 1 lemon, juiced
- 6 garlic cloves, minced
- 1 Tbsp dried oregano
- Salt and pepper, to taste
- Minced parsley for garnish

DIRECTIONS

1. Preheat the oven to 400°F.
2. In a 9x13-inch baking dish, add the olive oil, chicken stock, lemon juice, garlic cloves, oregano, and salt and pepper to taste. Whisk to combine. Add the potatoes and toss them in the sauce, then place them in an even layer.
3. Transfer to the oven and bake for 1 hour, stirring every 20 minutes. Remove from the oven once the potatoes are golden and the liquid has evaporated.
4. Serve and top with parsley.

Potato Leek Soup

This book wouldn't be complete without one of the best soups of all time: potato leek soup. I feel like this soup is often overlooked in favor of more popular options, but it is delicious and perfect on a cold day. So I say justice for potato leek soup! It deserves a spot among the best soups out there.

INGREDIENTS

- 2 Tbsp olive oil
- 3 leeks, white part only, finely chopped
- 1 onion, finely chopped
- Salt and pepper, to taste
- 5 garlic cloves, minced
- 1 cup dry white wine
- 1 lb russet potatoes, medium diced
- 1 quart chicken stock
- 1 standard sachet:
  - 1 bay leaf
  - 3 sprigs thyme
  - 10 peppercorns
  - 10 parsley stems
- 1 cup heavy cream or coconut cream
- Minced chives for garnish

DIRECTIONS

1. Heat olive oil in a stockpot and sauté the onions and leeks, seasoning with salt as you go, until translucent. This takes around 5-8 minutes. Once cooked, add the minced garlic and cook for another 2 minutes, until fragrant.
2. Stir in the white wine and scrape up any brown bits from the bottom of the pot. Bring to a simmer and reduce the liquid by half.
3. Increase the heat to medium-high and add the potatoes, stock, sachet, salt, and pepper. Bring to a simmer, cover with a lid, and cook for 20 minutes, or until the potatoes are fork-tender. Discard the sachet.
4. Purée the soup in batches in a blender or with an immersion blender. Stir in the cream and chives. Check for seasoning, then serve and enjoy!

Aloo Gobi

If you have never heard of Aloo Gobi, you can thank me now for introducing you to one of the best Indian dishes. Aloo Gobi translates to "potato cauliflower." It is an Indian vegetarian dish that is packed with aromatic spices, tomatoes, and vegetables stewed together.

INGREDIENTS

- 3 gold potatoes, cut into 1-inch cubes
- 1 cauliflower, cut into small florets
- 3 Tbsp oil
- 1 onion, diced
- Salt, to taste
- 1-inch piece of ginger, grated
- 6 garlic cloves, grated
- ½ tsp cumin
- ½ tsp turmeric powder
- 1 tsp coriander powder
- ½ tsp chili powder
- ½ tsp garam masala
- 1.5 cups canned tomato puree
- ½ cup chicken stock
- ½ lime, juiced
- Cilantro, for garnish

DIRECTIONS

1. Bring a pot of water to a boil and add a generous amount of salt. Boil the potatoes for 7 minutes, or until cooked through. Remove them and let them dry.
2. In the same pot, boil the cauliflower for 3 minutes, until fork-tender. Strain and dry. Set aside.
3. In a large sauté pan over medium heat, add the oil. Once warmed, add the onions and sauté until translucent, around 5-8 minutes, salting as you go. Once cooked through, add the ginger, garlic, and spices, and toast until fragrant, around 3 minutes.
4. Stir in the tomato puree and chicken stock and bring to a low simmer. Season with salt to taste and simmer for 10 minutes, or until the sauce has thickened and become flavorful.
5. Stir in the potatoes and cauliflower to coat them with the sauce. Cook for another 5 minutes to heat through.
6. Stir in the fresh lime juice, serve, and top with cilantro. Enjoy!

Aloo Tikka

SERVES: 6

Aloo tikka is a popular Indian appetizer made from spiced and pan-fried potato patties. It is essentially mashed potatoes with a variety of Indian spices, coated in starch, and fried, so you know it's going to be good!

INGREDIENTS

- 4 large russet potatoes, peeled and cut into 2-inch cubes
- Salt, to taste
- ¼ cup rice flour
- 1 jalapeño, minced
- 1-inch piece of ginger, grated
- 5 garlic cloves, grated
- 1 tsp chili powder
- 1 tsp turmeric powder
- 1 tsp cumin powder
- ½ tsp coriander powder
- ¼ cup cilantro, minced
- ½ cup cornstarch
- Avocado oil, for frying

DIRECTIONS

1. Fill a large pot with water and bring it to a boil. Add the potatoes and season generously with salt. Boil for 12 minutes, or until the potatoes are fork-tender. Strain through a colander and return the potatoes to the empty pot over medium heat. Stir for 3-5 minutes to evaporate the water from the potatoes, then turn off the heat.
2. Run the potatoes through a potato ricer to achieve a smooth consistency. Refrigerate for 2 hours or until they are completely cooled.
3. Once the potatoes are cooled, add the rice flour, jalapeño, ginger, garlic, chili powder, turmeric, cumin, coriander, and cilantro. Mix to combine and season with salt to taste. Make sure you taste it and add seasonings if needed! If it tastes bland now, it will taste bland after you fry up too!
4. Form the potato mixture into 2-inch flat patties. Coat each patty in cornstarch and set aside.
5. In a cast-iron skillet or frying pan, add avocado oil to a depth of about 1 inch. Turn the heat to medium, and once the oil is hot, work in batches to avoid overcrowding the pan. Fry the patties until golden brown on each side, about 3-5 minutes per side. Remove the patties once both sides are golden brown. Repeat with the remaining mixture and serve.

75

Papas Rellenas

If you like potato croquettes, just wait until you try these papas rellenas! They are a popular Latin American dish consisting of stuffed potato balls that are breaded and fried. You can fill them with just about anything, but here, I'm sticking to the Latin American theme with picadillo.

INGREDIENTS

Potato and Breading Ingredients:

- 4 large russet potatoes, peeled and cut into 2-inch cubes
- Salt and pepper, to taste
- ¼ cup cornstarch
- 2 eggs, whisked
- 1 cup gluten free flour or all-purpose flour
- 1 cup gluten free breadcrumbs or traditional breadcrumbs
- Avocado oil, for frying

Filling:

- ½ onion, diced
- Salt, to taste
- 4 garlic cloves, minced
- 1 lb ground beef
- 2 tbsp tomato paste
- 1 tsp cumin
- 1 tsp smoked paprika
- ½ cup green olives, diced
- ¼ cup cilantro, minced

DIRECTIONS

1. Fill a pot with water and bring it to a boil. Add the potatoes and season generously with salt. Boil for 12 minutes, or until the potatoes are fork-tender. Strain through a colander and return the potatoes to the empty pot over medium heat. Stir for 3-5 minutes to evaporate the water from the potatoes, then turn off the heat.
2. Run the potatoes through a potato ricer to form a mash. Season with salt and pepper, and mix in the cornstarch. Set aside.
3. In a large sauté pan over medium heat, add 1 tbsp of avocado oil. Once warm, add the onion and sauté until translucent, salting as you go. Once cooked, add the garlic and sauté for another 2 minutes until fragrant.
4. Add the ground beef and cook until browned and cooked through, salting as you go. This takes around 10 minutes.
5. Add the tomato paste, cumin, and smoked paprika to coat the beef. Sauté for another 5 minutes. Turn off the heat and mix in the olives and cilantro.
6. Prepare the breading station: In one bowl, add the flour; in another, add the breadcrumbs; and in a third bowl, mix the eggs with 2 tbsp of water to make the egg wash. Line a sheet tray with parchment paper and set aside.

Papas Rellenas

7. Stuff the potatoes: Take a portion of the mashed potatoes and flatten it in your hand. Place a spoonful of the meat filling in the center and encase it with the mashed potatoes, forming a ball or oval shape. Coat each ball first in the egg wash, then in the flour, back in the egg wash, and finally in the breadcrumbs. Place on the sheet tray and repeat with the remaining mixture.
8. Refrigerate for 2 hours so the balls will hold their shape.
9. Add avocado oil to a heavy-bottomed pot for frying and bring it up to 350°F. Working in batches, fry 2-3 balls at a time until they are golden brown, about 3-4 minutes.
10. Remove and drain on paper towels or a roasting rack over a sheet tray. Repeat with the remaining balls.
    Serve and enjoy!

Sweet Potatoes

Brown Butter & Sage Sweet Potato Puree

I prefer sweet potato mash over regular mashed potatoes. Now, hear me out. Most sweet potato mash is filled with marshmallows and brown sugar, and it's just too damn sweet. This sweet potato mash uses only yams and brown butter for the perfect balance of sweet and savory.

INGREDIENTS

- 1.5 lb yams
- ¼ cup butter
- 3 sprigs sage
- Salt, to taste

DIRECTIONS

1. Preheat the oven to 425°F.
2. Line a baking sheet with foil and then parchment paper. Add the sweet potatoes and poke with a fork 3-5 times so steam can escape. Bake in the oven for 45-60 minutes, until the sweet potatoes are cooked through and soft.
3. While the potatoes are in the oven make the brown butter. Place the butter in the saucepan or skillet over medium heat. Stir as the butter melts, it will start to foam, and you'll hear a sizzling sound. Add the sage and stir until the butter starts to brown, it will smell nutty and the browned bits will sink to the bottom. Remove from the heat and pour into a heat proof container.
4. Slice the potatoes open with a knife and remove the skin. Remove the flesh from the skin and place in a food processor or high powered blender. Blend the potatoes until they are smooth. While blending, pour in the butter until desired consistency is reached. You may not use all of the butter. Season with salt and serve!

Sweet Potato Casserole

If you think marshmallows should be in a sweet potato casserole... are you okay? Just kidding! But much like pineapple on pizza, marshmallows don't deserve to be a topping. Instead, try this delicious nutty topping that is much more balanced and adds a nice crunch.

INGREDIENTS

Potatoes:

- 3 large yams
- 2 large eggs
- ¼ cup coconut milk, just the cream
- 1 tsp salt
- 2 tsp cinnamon

Toppings:

- 1½ cups pecans
- ½ cup gluten-free flour or all-purpose flour
- ¼ cup coconut sugar
- ½ tsp salt
- 1 tsp cinnamon
- 3 Tbsp coconut oil

DIRECTIONS

1. Preheat the oven to 425°F.
2. Line a baking sheet with foil and place parchment paper on top. Add the sweet potatoes and poke them all over with a fork (this prevents them from exploding in the oven due to steam). Bake in the oven for 45 to 60 minutes, until the sweet potatoes are cooked through and fork-tender. Remove from the oven and slice open to cool slightly. Decrease the oven temperature to 400°F.
3. Scoop the flesh of the sweet potatoes into a food processor and blend until smooth. Pulse in the eggs, coconut milk, salt, and cinnamon until well combined. Transfer the mixture into a 9x9 baking dish and smooth out the top.
4. Clean out the food processor, then add the pecans. Pulse the pecans until they are crumbly and in small pieces. Add the pecans to a clean bowl along with the remaining topping ingredients. Mix with a spatula to combine. Sprinkle the topping evenly over the sweet potato mixture in the baking dish.
5. Cover the dish with foil and bake in the oven for 25 minutes. Remove the foil and bake for an additional 10 minutes.
6. Remove from the oven and cool for 10 minutes before serving. Enjoy!

Cinnamon Sweet Potato Wedges

This is hands down the potato recipe I make the most in my day-to-day life. I prepare these at least twice a week for dinner and have been doing so for the past two years. I never get sick of it. The cinnamon and brown sugar enhance the sweetness of Japanese sweet potatoes and caramelize to create a delicious crust. These are a must try!

INGREDIENTS

- 3 large Japanese sweet potatoes
- 2 Tbsp coconut oil
- Salt, to taste
- 1 tsp cinnamon
- 1 Tbsp brown sugar

DIRECTIONS

1. Preheat the oven to 400°F.
2. Cut the sweet potatoes into large wedges and place them in a bowl.
3. Add the coconut oil, salt, cinnamon, and brown sugar to the bowl, and stir to evenly coat the sweet potatoes.
4. Place the sweet potatoes on a parchment-lined sheet tray, ensuring there is space between each wedge. Transfer to the oven and bake for 20 minutes.
5. After 20 minutes, flip the potatoes over and bake for an additional 10 minutes.
6. Remove from the oven and serve immediately.

Sweet Potato Salad

SERVES: 6-8

There is nothing I hate more than a traditional potato salad. I know, I know, that sounds crazy! But a sweet potato salad is a whole other story—I can't get enough of it! I think it has much more interesting flavors that hold their own against mayo, unlike white potatoes, which often fall flat.

INGREDIENTS

- 1 lb yams, cut into 1-inch cubes
- 1 lb Japanese sweet potatoes, cut into 1-inch cubes
- 4 eggs
- 2 tbsp mustard seeds
- ⅓ cup + 2 tbsp apple cider vinegar
- ½ cup dill pickles, chopped
- ½ cup dill, minced
- ½ cup chives, minced
- 1 Tbsp Dijon mustard
- ¼ cup mayo

DIRECTIONS

1. Bring a large steamer pot to a boil. Add the potatoes to the steamer section and steam for 10 minutes.
2. After steaming the potatoes, remove them from the steamer and set aside.
3. In the same steamer pot, steam the eggs for 11 minutes. Once the 11 minutes are up, shock the eggs in an ice water bath to stop the cooking. Once they are cooled, peel and halve the eggs, then set aside.
4. In a small pan over medium heat, add the mustard seeds and ¼ cup of apple cider vinegar. Cover with a lid and cook until all of the liquid is absorbed by the mustard seeds. Turn off the heat and set aside.
5. In a bowl, combine the mustard seeds, herbs, pickles, remaining apple cider vinegar, mayo, and mustard. Mix with a spatula and adjust seasoning to taste.
6. Add the potatoes to the bowl and evenly coat them with the dressing.
7. Transfer to a serving bowl and top with the eggs. Serve at room temperature or chilled!

Purple Pommes Annna

This is a fun twist on traditional Pommes Anna by using purple potatoes. Purple potatoes are unique in being starchy and low in moisture, which makes them perfect for a delicious Pommes Anna. If you're looking to add a pop of color to your table, this is it!

INGREDIENTS

- 4 large purple sweet potatoes
- ¼ cup clarified butter or oil, melted
- Salt and pepper, to taste
- 3 garlic cloves, grated
- 2 tsp Italian seasoning

DIRECTIONS

1. Preheat the oven to 400°F.
2. Peel the potatoes and thinly slice them on a mandolin; aim for slices as thin as possible. Add the slices to a bowl and coat them with melted butter or oil, salt, pepper, grated garlic, and Italian seasoning. Mix well to ensure the potatoes are evenly coated.
3. Arrange the potatoes in a nonstick pan or cast iron skillet, layering some butter or oil in the pan first. I like to arrange them in circles, starting in the middle. Do one layer at a time, continuing until you run out of potatoes. Top the potatoes with parchment paper, then place a heavy, oven-safe object, such as a pot, on top. The object helps press the potatoes down, creating a great crust and more even cooking.
4. Bake in the oven for 25 minutes. Remove from the oven, take off the weight and parchment paper, and return the pan to the oven for another 15 minutes to brown the top.
5. Remove from the oven and flip the dish onto a plate. Let it sit for 10 minutes to cool slightly. Slice and serve! I like to sprinkle some flaky salt or herbs on top as well!

Sweet Potato Sheperd's Pie

Although the traditional Shepherd's pie with a white potato topping is a classic, this sweet potato version adds a little oomph. It's the perfect casserole for sweet potato lovers.

INGREDIENTS

- 2.5 lbs sweet potatoes or yams, peeled and halved
- Salt and pepper, to taste
- Avocado oil
- ½ yellow onion, diced
- 5 carrots, diced
- 1 celery rib, diced
- 4 garlic cloves, minced
- 1 tsp thyme
- 1 tsp rosemary
- 1.5 lbs ground beef
- ¼ cup tomato paste
- 1 Tbsp gluten-free flour
- ½ cup beef or chicken stock

DIRECTIONS

1. Preheat the oven to 375°F.
2. In a pot of salted water, boil the potatoes for 30 minutes, or until fork tender. Remove them and place on a sheet tray to dry in the oven for 10 minutes. Mash the potatoes by putting them through a ricer, smooth with a spatula, and season with salt and pepper. Set the mash aside.
3. In a large pan over medium heat, add oil and sauté the onion, carrots, and celery until translucent, salting as you go. Once cooked through, add the garlic and sauté for another 2 minutes. Add the rosemary, thyme, and ground beef, and continue to sauté, salting and peppering as you go. Once the beef is browned, add the tomato paste to coat the beef and sauté for 3 minutes. Sprinkle with flour and coat the beef. Add the stock, stir, and simmer for 3-5 minutes until thickened. Turn off the heat.
4. Transfer the beef mixture to an 8x8 casserole dish or pie pan. Using a spatula, spread it into an even layer. Top with the mashed potatoes and smooth them into an even layer. Use a fork to create a decorative design.
5. Transfer to the oven and bake for 30 minutes. After 30 minutes, broil for 5 minutes to brown the top.
6. Remove from the oven and cool for 10 minutes before serving.

Sweet Potato Gnocchi

Sweet Potato Gnocchi

I can't even begin to describe how good this sweet potato gnocchi is. It's mildly sweet, beautifully colored, and perfect when paired with a brown butter sage sauce! It is worth every second it takes to make.

INGREDIENTS

- 2 lbs yams
- 2 cups gluten free 1-to-1 flour or 00 flour
- 1 tsp salt

DIRECTIONS

1. Preheat the oven to 375°F.
2. Poke the potatoes all over with a fork. Place them on a sheet tray and bake for 45 minutes to 1 hour, or until they are soft, fork-tender, and cooked through.
3. Peel the skin off the potatoes and discard it. Push the potatoes through a ricer. If you don't have a ricer, push them through a fine mesh strainer.
4. Dust your countertop with flour. Place the riced potatoes flat on the surface and coat with 2 cups of flour. Mix together with your hands, adding more flour if needed. Add the salt and knead the dough just until a ball forms. Cut into quarters. Add more flour if the dough is too wet.
5. Working with one section at a time, roll the dough out with your hands until it is about 1/2 inch thick. Using a bench scraper or knife, cut into small pieces. Set aside and dust with flour to prevent sticking.
6. Cook the gnocchi. Bring a large pot of salted water to a boil. Add the gnocchi in batches, avoiding overcrowding the pot. Bring the water back to a low boil. Once the gnocchi floats to the top, remove them with a slotted spoon.
7. Finish in sauce and serve.

Sweet Potato Chips

These were my favorite recipe from my first cookbook, The Basics of Cooking, so I obviously had to include them in this cookbook as well! Even though it may seem extra to make your own chips, it is totally worth it. They are sweet, crispy, and have the perfect crunch.

INGREDIENTS

- 3 skinny yams
- 4-6 cups avocado oil, for frying
- Salt, to taste

DIRECTIONS

1. Using a mandolin set to a very thin setting, slice the sweet potatoes into thin chips and set aside.
2. In a Dutch oven or cast iron skillet, heat the oil to 375°F. Working in batches, fry the sweet potato chips for 3-5 minutes, or until they rise and are golden brown and crispy. Using a spider, remove the chips from the pot and transfer them to a bowl. Salt immediately and serve.

Sweet Potato Fries

If I'm at a restaurant and sweet potato fries are on the menu, there's a 100% chance I'm ordering them. But half the time, they turn out soggy and disappointing. I wish I could share the steps in this recipe with those restaurants because these fries are guaranteed to be the crispiest!

INGREDIENTS

- 3 yams, peeled and cut into fry shapes
- 4-6 cups avocado oil, for frying
- 1 cup cornstarch
- ¾ cup club soda, refrigerated
- Salt, to taste
- 1 tsp garlic powder
- ¼ tsp smoked paprika

DIRECTIONS

1. Add the cut yams to bowls of ice-cold water and soak for 30 minutes to remove the starches. After 30 minutes, pat dry with paper towels.
2. Heat the oil in a pot over the stove to 375°F.
3. While the oil is heating, prepare the batter. Whisk the cornstarch and club soda together in a bowl until smooth. Add the fries to the batter and coat them evenly. Allow excess batter to drip off by placing the fries on a roasting rack set over a sheet tray.
4. Once the oil is hot, work in batches to fry the fries until golden brown, about 6-9 minutes.
5. Remove the fries from the oil and place them in a bowl. Immediately season with salt, garlic powder, and smoked paprika. Repeat with the remaining fries.
6. Serve immediately and enjoy!

Rendang Kentang

Rendang Kentang

Rendang Kentang is an Indonesian coconut curry dish that is absolutely delicious. I've put my own twist on it, but it still retains the essence of the traditional dish. It's packed with strong herbs, aromatics, and spices that pack a punch.

INGREDIENTS

Spice Blend Ingredients:

- 2 shallots, peeled and thinly sliced
- 4 cloves garlic, thinly sliced
- 2 serrano peppers, seeded and sliced
- 1-inch piece of ginger, thinly sliced
- 1 lemongrass stalk, white part only, thinly sliced
- 1 tsp coriander powder
- 1 tsp cumin powder
- 2 Tbsp avocado oil, or more as needed for blending

Other Ingredients:

- 1 can coconut milk
- 2 Japanese sweet potatoes, peeled and cut into bite-sized chunks
- Salt, to taste
- 2 Tbsp coconut sugar
- 2 tsp fish sauce
- ½ lime, juiced
- Cilantro sprigs, for garnish

DIRECTIONS

1. Blend all of the spice blend ingredients in a blender until smooth, adding oil and water as needed to achieve a smooth consistency.
2. In a pot over medium heat, add 1 tbsp avocado oil and warm it. Add the spice paste and sauté until fragrant, stirring frequently, for about 2 minutes.
3. Pour in the coconut milk, stirring well to combine with the spice paste. Bring the mixture to a simmer and season with salt to taste.
4. Add the potatoes, coconut sugar, fish sauce, and lime juice. Stir to coat the potatoes with the coconut mixture. Bring the mixture to a simmer, then reduce the heat to low. Allow it to simmer gently, stirring occasionally to prevent sticking, until the potatoes are tender and the sauce has thickened, about 10-20 minutes.
5. Continue cooking until the coconut milk is well absorbed by the potatoes. Once the potatoes are cooked through and very soft, turn off the heat. Adjust the seasoning if needed.
6. Serve topped with cilantro leaves.

Aji De Papas

Aji de Papas is a traditional Peruvian dish that stews potatoes in a creamy, spicy sauce. Any recipe that uses my two favorite ingredients, sweet potatoes and peanuts, is a winner.

INGREDIENTS

For the Potatoes:
- 2 large yams, peeled and cut into bite-sized chunks
- Salt, to taste

Ingredients for the Sauce:
- 1 cup peanuts, unsalted and roasted
- 4 garlic cloves, minced
- 2 Tbsp aji amarillo paste (Peruvian yellow chili paste)
- 1 Tbsp avocado oil
- 1 onion, diced
- 1 cup chicken stock
- 1 tsp cumin, ground
- 1 lime, juiced
- Salt and pepper, to taste

For Garnish:
- 2 hard-boiled eggs, thinly sliced
- ½ cup black olives, sliced
- ¼ cup cilantro, minced

DIRECTIONS

1. Peel and cut the potatoes into bite-sized chunks. Bring a double boiler to a boil and add the potatoes. Steam for 8-10 minutes until fork-tender but not mushy. Set aside.
2. Prepare the Peanut Sauce. In a blender or food processor, combine the roasted peanuts, minced garlic, and aji amarillo paste with a few tablespoons of the stock. Blend until you have a smooth peanut mixture.
3. In a large pan, heat the avocado oil over medium heat. Once hot, add the onions and cook until translucent, salting as you go. This takes about 5 minutes.
4. Add the peanut mixture to the pan and stir well. Pour in the chicken stock, add the cumin, lime juice, and season with salt and pepper. Simmer the sauce for about 5-10 minutes, allowing it to thicken.
5. Add the boiled potatoes to the peanut sauce. Gently stir to coat the potatoes with the sauce. Simmer for an additional 5-10 minutes, allowing the flavors to combine. Season to taste.
6. Transfer the Aji de Papas to a serving dish. Garnish with sliced eggs, olives, and cilantro, and enjoy!

Daigaku Imo

Daigaku Imo is a popular Japanese potato dish usually eaten as a snack or dessert. Japanese sweet potatoes are roasted and then candied with a soy sauce and sugar glaze to bring out their natural sweetness. The umami from the soy sauce mixed with the sugar and sesame seeds creates a unique potato dish that you won't be able to stop eating.

INGREDIENTS

- 2 large Japanese sweet potatoes, washed and cut into 2-inch cubes
- Avocado oil
- Salt, to taste
- 3 Tbsp tamari
- ¼ cup mirin
- ¼ cup granulated sugar
- 2 tsp sesame oil
- Black sesame seeds for garnish

DIRECTIONS

1. Preheat the oven to 400°F.
2. Add the sweet potatoes to a bowl and coat evenly with avocado oil and a small amount of salt. Spread them onto a parchment-lined sheet tray and bake for 20 minutes.
3. Remove from the oven, flip the sweet potatoes over, and bake for another 10 minutes. Remove from the oven and set aside.
4. In a large sauté pan, add the tamari, mirin, sugar, and sesame oil. Simmer over low heat and reduce for 3 minutes to make a thick glaze.
5. Once the sauce has thickened, add the sweet potatoes and cook for another 5 minutes to glaze them.
6. Serve and garnish with black sesame seeds. Enjoy!

Thank You

Thank you so much for your support in buying this book! It's people like you who allow me to live my dream. I am forever grateful for the opportunity to share my knowledge and passion for cooking with the world. I hope you enjoy these potato recipes as much as I do. Happy cooking!

ABOUT KELLY

Kelly is a professional chef based in South Orange County, specializing in gluten-free diets, niche cuisines, and allergen-free cooking. Her goal is to teach others how to become better home cooks while also serving her community through events and personal chef services.

Kelly received professional training at the Culinary Institute of America, where she acquired the techniques and skills necessary to establish a solid foundation for her career. With over seven years of experience in professional kitchens and restaurants, she decided to start her own personal chef company, Kelly's Clean Kitchen, to work more closely with individuals and curate the best meals for them.

In recent years, she has grown an online community through her social channels by teaching people how to cook through educational videos. This success led her to self-publish her first cookbook, The Basics of Cooking, which serves as a crash course in the fundamentals of cooking. She continues to leverage her following and reach to help others learn how to cook and have fun in the kitchen.